The Standard American Accent

Accent Reduction

Instruction on how American speakers stress

their words and produce their vowel sounds

copyright 2013

by Ivan Borodin

Introduction

I've seen people sweat from just talking about their speech, dangerously close to quitting class. If there's nobody to blame for having an accent, then why do they want to blame themselves?

And there are some foreign speakers who ignore the issue, trusting blindly that time spent in English as a Second Language class will magically transform their accent. Faith is fine, but you can't be starving in a closet and just pray for a sandwich.

The jury has only begun deliberating. Finger-comb your hair, slap some color into your cheeks, and start going through this manual.

You can keep your practice within the walls of your home and the confines of your privacy.

If you get stuck, take a breather. Sometimes it's best to let the results come to you. In a very tangible way, we can't control our speech. We certainly can't *see* the muscles involved, and parts of our bodies such as the soft palate are difficult to even describe.

Yet experience has shown me that spending time with source materials, in this case the following program, will deliver clear speech in a remarkably short time.

Understanding the American Stress

Pattern

Repeat the following words. Notice how they fall in pitch.

have   *low*   *do*

Now say these words, placing the emphasis on the underlined syllable.

<u>au</u>*to*   <u>ba</u>*by*   <u>tar</u>*get*   <u>win</u>*dow*

In that last group of two-syllable words, the stress falls on the first part of the word. Americans emphasize their words by going downward in pitch on the stressed syllable. When an American stresses a word, they move downward in pitch *within* the stressed syllable. This is in direct contrast to the majority of the world's languages, which tend to rise upward in pitch on stressed syllables.

cam<u>paign</u>   *gui<u>tar</u>*   *be<u>sides</u>*

<u>a</u>venue   *<u>dang</u>erous*

lo<u>cat</u>ion   *in<u>sur</u>ance*   *in<u>vit</u>ed*

One misconception is that Americans stress the beginning of all words.

In the next group, the stress falls on both the first and third syllables. Notice how when syllables are stressed, the speaker goes down in pitch.

disappoint   *introduce*   *entertain*

On words with several syllables, you need to identify which syllable or syllables receive emphasis.

ceremony   *television*   *temporary*

a<u>rith</u>metic   psy<u>cho</u>logy   e<u>mer</u>gency

Double-stressed words occur very often in American English.

<u>re</u>cog<u>ni</u>tion   *<u>ob</u>ser<u>va</u>tion*

<u>edu</u>cation   *<u>ra</u>tionali<u>za</u>tion*

<u>al</u>pha<u>be</u>tical   *en<u>cy</u>clo<u>pe</u>dia*

<u>au</u>to<u>bio</u>gra<u>phi</u>cal (three stresses)

Americans move downward in pitch on every stressed syllable. Become aware of where the emphasis is and emphasize very clearly by going downward in pitch on stressed syllables. During this program, underlines will be used to point out when a syllable is stressed, in order to remind the listener to go down in pitch.

American Vowels

Stressed sounds descend in pitch. The five vowel sounds that demonstrate this falling in pitch are **A, E, I, O, U.** Notice how the sounds go downward in pitch. After the following sentences, please repeat the phrases, and try to make the stressed sounds descend in pitch.

7

The Long A

You should have *made* your pre̲sence known.

Your sec̲ret is *safe* with me.

You, miss, are no *la̲dy.*

Please don't *take* ad̲va̲ntage of me.

This is a *change* for a free-spirited per̲son.

She works on a free̲lance *ba̲sis.*

I need a *sa̲fety* net.

The fina̲ncial advisor *gave* her a *sa̲vings* plan.

The emplo̲y̲ment *situa̲tion rema̲ins sha̲ky.*

Paul is not *ma̲king* any ef̲fort.

Li̲nda fo̲llowed Pat's *reco̲mmenda̲tions.*

They've ta̲ken the first steps.

It was a *great* step <u>for</u>ward.

<u>*May*</u>*be* I could *make* a few points.

When it's cooked enough, it should be <u>*flaky*</u>.

That was a *great play*.

It's been <u>*raining*</u> in San *Diego*.

<u>*Yes*</u>*terday* I *baked* my first *great cake*.

I saw the <u>mov</u>ie "<u>*Cabaret*</u>" in a French *café*.

<u>*May*</u>*be* I could *name* the <u>*Statesman's*</u> *age*.

You'll *pay* for the <u>*danger*</u> of your <u>*misbehavior*</u>.

Say that you'll *trade* your <u>*savings*</u> for the *case*.

When Americans use an imperative, command, or suggestion, they move downward in pitch.

Say that you'll do it.

Do that.

Bel<u>iev</u>e what I tell you.

The *ma<u>j</u>or* was *re<u>lat</u>ed* to the guy *backstage*.

He was *<u>able</u>* to drive in the *rain* be<u>fore</u> the dam *gave way*.

I *ac<u>quaint</u>ed* myself with the *<u>ed</u>ucator*.

When Americans are very emphatic, they curve down even more in pitch.

There's *no way* I would <u>*ever*</u> do that.

So what? It's *my life.*

11

The Long I

why, quite, sur<u>prise</u>, invite, while, sign, guy

The I sound must begin with a clear 'AH' sound (for example, *why, die, lie*) and descend sharply in pitch.

I've been <u>*trying*</u> to do what's *right*.

<u>*Tonight*</u> was the first *time I've* been out.

I think if he was *al<u>ive</u>, I'd* do <u>eve</u>rything I could to meet him.

I don't *like* that *kind* of talk.

I'm <u>*trying*</u> to do what's *right*.

It was his <u>*finest*</u> hour.

You're a *fine* man.

They would suffer *side-effects* for decades.

A new *kind* of *society* would emerge.

Our *mighty* leader was going to be *denied.*

Such a *trial* could alter history.

Her approach to personal *finance* bordered on the reckless.

His own *child* is grown.

Helen commits to a disciplined *retirement* plan.

He *advised* her how to place her holdings.

Frank *decided* to tackle one credit card at a *time.*

He lost his *license nine* years ago.

He noticed the sunlit *sky* of *blinding light.*

It was a once in a *lifetime* occurrence.

Officials stewed *silently* <u>ov</u>er the e<u>ve</u>nt.

The <u>numb</u>ers con<u>tin</u>ue to *de<u>cline</u>*.

Should re<u>lig</u>ion *guide* be<u>hav</u>ior?

The <u>qual</u>ity of *life* is im<u>port</u>ant.

He played for *O<u>hio</u>* State.

What's your *sign?* A <u>class</u>ic *line*.

...and now, a <u>happy</u> *sur<u>prise</u>* for all of us.

How *kind* of you to re<u>mem</u>ber.

You can <u>al</u>so have *mine.*

This *might* be the *right* <u>mo</u>ment.

Climb into your car and *drive* a<u>way</u>.

It's not a <u>pret</u>ty *sight,* is it?

The <u>pic</u>tures came to *life.*

We can *tie* the two <u>ideas</u> to<u>geth</u>er.

14

The Long U

do, suitable.

I've lost my *shoe.*

I just bought a *new toothbrush.*

And the same is *true* for *you, too.*

He *introduced* a bill.

It was the largest *opportunity* he has ever been offered.

They pressed for expansion despite *community* resistance.

The plan has never received city *approval.*

It was a *move* timed to *smooth* the way.

They *accused* Wilson of *fueling* racial tension.

There's no *use doing that.*

The Long O

The wind is _blowing cold snow._

The ho<u>tel</u> by the <u>_ocean_</u> is <u>_open_</u> in <u>_November._</u>

I took the _dough_ out of the _bowl._

Your lips should form a W at the end of words that end with a long O. Some dictionaries even add a W at the tail of phonetic transcriptions of these words:

dough, go, low, know

I _hope_ I can _go home_ to<u>morr</u>ow.

She _rowed_ the _boat_ <u>_over_</u> the <u>_ocean._</u>

Joan was <u>_bloated_</u> <u>af</u>ter <u>eat</u>ing the _roast._

She called *home*, *hoping* for a big *loan*.

Only the *lonely* enjoy flying *solo* *over* the South *Pole*.

The thirty-year *old* house is *sold*.

Don't catch a *cold*.

How are you *holding* up?

I was *jolted* when you entered unexpectedly.

She was *told* not to *hold* the baby.

The Long E

Keep it. I don't *need* it.

The long E should resonate off the lower teeth. It is a sharp, bright sound.

All the <u>*teena*</u>*gers* are at the *beach* to<u>day</u>.

She <u>wan</u>ted to *bleach* her *teeth*.

My *feet* are <u>kill</u>ing me.

The <u>*meeting*</u> will be held by the large *tree*.

His quest for <u>*freedom*</u> was quite an *or<u>deal</u>*.

That was a <u>*devious deed*</u>.

It's a <u>*tedious*</u> task to *clean* the re<u>frig</u>erator.

I'm *ex<u>tremely</u> re<u>lieved</u>* that he <u>*agreed*</u> to *meet* the whole *team*.

I *teased* her, <u>cal</u>ling her *de<u>ceit</u>ful*.

Clues to Determining Syllable Stress

We've now examined the *obvious curves* of the American Accent, those five basic vowels that most clearly demonstrate the dropping in pitch within stressed syllables.

How do you know when to move the pitch downward? What part of the word receives the emphasis?

Here are a few clues.

The -ION ending

When there is an -ION ending, place the emphasis on the syllable directly before it.

union - stress the long U

negotiation - This double-stressed word is an example of both the -ION guideline and the American's tendency to stress more than one syllable in polysyllabic words.

They're spending *millions* of dollars on public *relations*.

We agreed on greater *cooperation*.

We're attempting to reach an early *decision*.

He completed the *application*.

There is a low risk of *prosecution*.

That only added to his *humiliation*.

He was against the entire *foundation*.

He created the perfect *conditions*.

I found a charitable *organization*.

They are processing his *application*.

. There was too much *speculation* surrounding the crime.

I don't have time for *contradictions*.

It was one of the major *obsessions* of his life.

21

The -ING rule

When a word ends with -ING, unless it is a single syllable word, it will not receive stress on the -ING ending.

In the word *trying* you'll only stress the first part.

In the word *demonstrating* you'll stress *dem*, the first syllable.

In the word *negotiating*, you'll stress *go*, but you won't stress the *ing*.

The *ing* ending will never receive stress, unless the word itself is based in *ing*, like *sing*, *thing* or *wing*.

> The *wings* of a dove.
>
> Within that phrase, the word *wings* will be stressed. Otherwise, the *ing* will not receive stress.

How much *shopping* can a woman do?

The book has been *flying* off store shelves.

He was excellent at *creating* beauty with light.

We've been *watching* what we eat.

I'm *trying* to take walks after dinner.

The wrong man might be *doing* time.

I'll tell you *everything* you want to hear.

It's *going* to be a couple of days.

We really enjoyed *working* together.

23

The Soft Palate

The soft palate is a delicate piece of cartilage between the roof of the mouth and the uvula (that fleshy extension that hangs in the back of the mouth). If you put your finger in your mouth and touch your upper teeth, then reach and touch the gum behind the upper teeth, then continue to reach up and back, past the roof of your mouth, it grows wetter and softer as you go back.

The very large, soft portion of flesh that exists between the roof of your mouth and your uvula is called the soft palate.

> When Americans stress words, they tend to move that soft piece of flesh downward and forward. This is demonstrated in the words *cup, cop* and *get*.

Remember to keep the pitch of the words moving downwards, but now add this muscular movement.

The Short U

run, brothers, hunting, stuntman, stumble, mud, love

The *stuntman stumbles* and *tumbles* in the *mud*.

A *mother loves* her *son*.

I'll come *over* on *Sunday* if it's *sunny*.

He *won some money, but* not *enough*.

The *drunk mumbled something* into his *cup*.

Southern hunters used *clubs* and lived in *huts*.

Hundreds and *hundreds* of *ducks* came from the *river*.

What a *wonderful country*.

There are so *many* different *cultures* in this *country*.

Put a cake in the *oven*.

Indulge her with the *luxury* of our bath collection.

I listened to an interview with a Buddhist *monk.*

He left the *jungle* in nineteen sixty three.

The organization would not release *results.*

She's so *lovely.*

He's a *bum, but* she says *nothing,* because he's her *son,* and she *loves* him.

One thing leads to *another.*

The music was *funky.*

It's not your *cup* of tea.

When the *sun comes up,* I have to be *up.*

The *lump sum* is incredibly large.

They *hugged* with tears in their eyes.

The Short O

I think they think I'm *involved* in something.

It could go as far up as the *mob*.

She'll *calm* you down.

I'd <u>bet</u>ter *watch* myself.

That's some *<u>con</u>cept*, huh?

Think about the *positive* things that have
<u>happ</u>ened to you.

I talked to your *mom* to<u>day</u>.

Ten <u>thous</u>and *dollars* just for <u>do</u>ing our *job*?

That's <u>very</u> *popular* at flea markets.

He *<u>apo</u>logizes* for <u>mess</u>ing you up.

She sings a two song *encore*.

Try to *stop* me.

I don't sup<u>pose</u> <u>an</u>yone is up at this *ungodly* hour.

He <u>stif</u>led his *re<u>sponse</u>* to the in<u>sul</u>ting *ob<u>serva</u>tion*.

The American R

Perhaps the most important aspect of the American accent is the American *hard R*. The American R is the only R worldwide that is considered a truly hard one. The Irish 'aaR' is close, but the American R is a fully retroflexed R.

The tip of the tongue moves back, points backward, flexes back, *retro*flexes, to create a very hard, throaty sound, as in the word *or*.

OR

OR is often pronounced when it appears in a word as 'or'.

for, or̲der, or̲dinary, short, cord, fork, rem̲orse, force.

However, there are exceptions:

word, work, worst, world, worm

OR is also produced during the 'ore' letter combination:

core, bef̲ore, res̲tored, more, shore

OR is also produced during the 'oor' combination:

door, floor

OR is also produced during the 'oar' combination:

oar, roar, soar

OR also appears when 'ar' follows a W on a stressed syllable:

war, warn, ward, toward, swarm, <u>war</u>rior

This is not the case when E follows 'war'

<u>war</u>ehouse, <u>hard</u>ware, stare

You need to create a very hard sound with the R: *warned, short-lived*

He's <u>never</u> <u>acted</u> like this *be<u>fore.</u>*

I saw all these <u>people</u> <u>try</u>ing to find *<u>or</u>der* in this world of com<u>plete</u> *dis<u>or</u>der.*

I will be *ex<u>plor</u>ing* that <u>sub</u>ject in this book.

The *four* of you are dis<u>tinct</u> from each other.

The Ad<u>mini</u><u>stra</u>tion Building was quite *or<u>dina</u>ry*.

It will be *re<u>stored</u>* <u>af</u>ter we pass through.

They moved <u>forw</u>ard at once.

This *door* is *more ornate* than the <u>othe</u>rs.

He felt the *<u>corn</u>ers* of his mouth twitch, as he thought that he should have been *warned*.

I <u>won</u>der what's his <u>drivi</u>ng *force*.

The e<u>stab</u>lishment must be put in *<u>ord</u>er* by *<u>morn</u>ing*.

She's a<u>bout</u> to have a new and *for<u>mi</u>dable* compe<u>ti</u>tor.

I must *warn* you that I will not do it.

There is <u>scarce</u>ly time to *re<u>cord</u>* these notes.

AR

AR is frequently produced when the letters 'ar' are together without an E following them:

star, car, Mars, bar, far, darn, guard, large, start, dark, arm, smart, re<u>mark</u>, charge

However, the following words are pronounced with different R vowels:

war, <u>back</u>ward, <u>for</u>ward, toward

The word *our* can be pronounced like *power*, but Americans frequently pronounce it with the AR sound:

I'm <u>go</u>ing to *our* car.

That <u>doesn</u>'t be<u>long</u> to you, it's *ours*.

It was *our* <u>on</u>ly chance to <u>fin</u>ally claim what was *ours*.

Our <u>meet</u>ing starts in two <u>min</u>utes.

His <u>feat</u>ures are *dark* and <u>rough</u>ened.

Please don't *start* with the *smart <u>remarks</u>*.

In your *heart* you know the <u>diff</u>erence, and you need to feed that *part* of you.

You and your mom should *start* <u>writ</u>ing <u>let</u>ters.

You <u>*startl*</u>*ed* me.

Are you <u>try</u>ing to give me a *heart* attack?

I'm still re<u>pair</u>ing the *<u>start</u>er* on this *car*.

He shot her a *harsh* glance and then left <u>ang</u>rily.

They <u>real</u>ly do have nice <u>carp</u>eting here.

The <u>Laun</u>dromat was *<u>sparsely</u>* <u>pop</u>ulated at that time of night.

In the *armed* <u>forc</u>es they have a thing called boot camp.

I <u>real</u>ly ap<u>prec</u>iate the help with the car.

AIR

AIR is often pronounced when 'ar' is followed by an E, Y or I.

care, scare, dare, spare, <u>bare</u>ly, <u>marry</u>, rare, a<u>ware</u>, <u>caring</u>, <u>sharing</u>

AIR appears during the 'air' combination:

fair, pair, upstairs

AIR *may* appear during the 'ere' and 'ear' combinations:

where, swear

But not always:

were, ear

I don't *care* what you think about him.

Where's your <u>un</u>cle?

What are you <u>do</u>ing *upstairs*?

How *dare* you spy on me?

I *swear* to you, I have no <u>idea</u> *where* she's gone.

Get the hard R in *where* without lingering on the word.

In the sentence:

I have no idea where she's gone.

You mustn't stop on the word:

I have no idea *wherrrre* she's gone.

All American sounds are short (less than a half a second long). In an effort to sound proper, some students of the American accent stretch out their sounds. Americans generally move quickly through their words.

He *apparently* has taken a trip to San Francisco.

Some of these trees look <u>pret</u>ty *scary*.

She *barely* sleeps.

I think it's *fair*.

She likes to walk *barefoot* on the beach.

The <u>can</u>didates were *primarily* <u>corp</u>orate <u>CEO</u>s.

Food was *scarce* at the time.

It was a <u>cit</u>y with a *flair* of <u>in</u>nocence.

> **The Three Major Aspects of the American Accent**
>
> *The dropping in pitch when syllables are stressed
>
> *The lowering of the soft palate as syllables are stressed
>
> *The curving of the American hard R

It is recommended that the student of the American Accent go back over this program numerous times to absorb all the vowel and consonant changes.

Keep in mind that learning an accent requires patience. Put the necessary time into it.

Thanks for doing the work. Best of luck with your American accent.

41

Final Notes

As you complete your first reading of this material, try not to view it with horror. There's a lot of information to process.

Also, try not to consider the author a mustache-twister who presented you a handful of spiders. Now that you are aware of what sounds you need to change, what remains is only a question of time and energy.

Perhaps you have doubts about your chances. Maybe you don't see your speech improving. As someone who has taught the subject for two decades, accent reduction isn't a controversial thing. It's a well-settled fact.

The author intends to make support for this publication available online. At the time of this writing, YouTube is the most popular site for posting videos that demonstrate chapters of this book.

To find online lessons in Accent Reduction, search **IvanBorodin** and/or **Accent Reduction** on YouTube.

43

The author recognizes the Internet as an evolving beast. Should another site become the leader in social media, please search for support for this book using the tags listed above.

About the Author

My students get tired of hearing this story, but it really happened.

As a young actor from New York City, I found myself getting verbally cuffed by casting directors over my thick accent. It was one big unavoidable mess, and I was unfortunately in the middle of it. The whole thing was a rain cloud over my acting career. I grew tired and distant.

I studied with several speech coaches, yet I often felt like I skipped a lesson somewhere, because the way they sounded didn't reflect what I heard in the media.

After learning the basics of the phonetic alphabet, I turned the volume up on my television and analyzed how Americans truly pronounce their vowels and consonants. This combination of book-learning and ruthless appraisal opened the doors to understanding the American accent.

My own accent became a virtual non-issue. I began coaching, then in the nineties I started as an instructor in the Los Angeles City College system. Nearly two decades later, the fundamentals of the American Accent are now at your disposal.

I work in television (I've appeared on *The District* and *Sabrina, the Teenage Witch*), but am available for coaching, both from my studio in Hollywood and via Skype worldwide.

Ivan Borodin

1626 N. Wilcox Avenue #490

Los Angeles, California 90028

IvanPresents@gmail.com

home (323) 319-4826

Skype handle: IvanBorodinUSA

Made in the USA
Lexington, KY
03 June 2014